Published in 2020 by The Rosen Publishing Group, Inc.
29 East 21st Street, New York, NY 10010

First Edition

Library of Congress Cataloging-in-Publication Data

Names: Rauf, Don, author.
Title: Careers in machine maintenance / Don Rauf.
Description: First edition. | New York : Rosen Publishing, 2020. |
Series: Makerspace careers | Audience: Grades 7–12. | Includes
bibliographical references and index.
Identifiers: LCCN 2018050169| ISBN 9781508188070 (library
bound) | ISBN 9781508188063 (paperback)
Subjects: LCSH: Machinery—Maintenance and repair—Voca-
tional guidance—Juvenile literature.
Classification: LCC TJ153 .R26 2020 | DDC 621.8/16023—dc23
LC record available at https://lccn.loc.gov/2018050169

Manufactured in China

CONTENTS

INTRODUCTION

What is the makerspace movement? Makerspaces are bringing people together to do hands-on creative and often technology-oriented projects. They are teaching people to build robots, fix bicycles, program gadgets, make model airplanes, use 3D printers, and more. The emphasis is on hands-on work and showing people that they can learn things that may at first seem beyond their grasp.

These makerspaces are perfect training grounds for those who want to pursue a career in machine maintenance. Machine mechanics and maintenance workers are in demand to keep all types of factory equipment and industrial machinery humming along and operating correctly. Young people can enter most of these careers with just a high school diploma, but having the hands-on experience working on repairs and fixing and building electronics, gadgets, engines, and other items can provide the real-life skills needed to be successful in this field.

Many people use electronic devices and machines, but they don't know how they operate. Maker groups give people a mindset so that they cannot only understand how things work, but they can make things themselves.

In 2018, students at the Moffitt Library Makerspace at University of California Berkeley designed a robot that could locate survivors in a disaster. A group of four students built a device that could identify human voice frequencies and then

Makerspaces often give students the opportunity to create projects with cutting-edge technology, such as 3D printers, which can produce three-dimensional objects by laying down successive layers of material.

give the direction indicating where the voices were coming from. The project helped students learn some very high-tech skills about circuit design, motor controls, and algorithms.

The students involved in the project said that the makerspace environment let them pool their talents, ideas, and resources. Plus the space gave them essential items like Arduino motors that run on simple computers and Raspberry Pis, which are tiny, inexpensive computers that can enable devices to perform all sorts of functions. In addition, makerspaces may provide soldering irons, wire clippers, oscilloscopes (for measuring electronic signals), and other helpful tools.

In an article in *Berkeley Library News*, one student maker said, "People are interested in doing cool projects, where they build stuff and it moves and can solve problems. But you can't do it on your own— you need a community. We get people to think about what they can make, because we have the resources for them to do it."

They sometimes take place in libraries, schools, and other spaces that available for public use. Their emphasis is on basic STEAM skills, which focus on Science, Technology, Engineering, Arts, and Math.

Makers are hobbyists, enthusiasts, and students or amateurs interested in innovation, creating new products, and producing value in the community. Through hands-on learning, makerspaces provide people with skills that can translate into successful careers. Some makers go on to become entrepreneurs and start companies.

CHAPTER ONE

MASTERING SKILLS THROUGH MAKING

Makerspaces are busy hives of production and activity. They make learning fun because you are actually constructing something and can see the end results. Students find makerspace programs in their schools, local libraries, colleges, churches, and community centers. In a sense, makerspaces are an evolution from the electric shops, wood shops, and automotive classes that more high schools once offered.

Sometimes, makerspaces are set up by nonprofit organizations or funded by private industry. At Familab in Longwood, Florida—not far from Disney World—young people are busy soldering and building circuitry. Sector67 in Madison, Wisconsin has students constructing their own flashlights and voice-activated LED lighting. Using programming, welding, and all sorts of electronics, the kids at Vocademy in Riverside, California, whip up all manner of robots. For careers in machine maintenance, you have

Like many makerspaces across the country, the Mt. Elliott Makerspace in Detroit gives children and teens the tools, guidance, and space to make things with their own two hands.

to understand the nuts and bolts of how things work, and that's exactly what these makerspaces do.

If you can't find a makerspace near you, you can always try to set up one on your own. Makerspaces.com and other websites provide many tips. A student may first want to inquire with their school administration to see what might be possible. A basic space will be equipped with electrical outlets, big empty tables where students can work, and a place to store tools and supplies. (First aid kits should always be on the premises as well!)

TOOLS AND TEACHERS

Markerspaces need to offer a variety of tools. Some are very simple and more craft-oriented with just scissors, glue, cardboard, and various art supplies. The ones that give skills for machine maintenance will have more advanced items. These may include batteries, copper foil tape (for learning about circuitry), LED lights, and circuits.

Many of these spaces, like the Artisan's Asylum, in Somerville, Massachusetts, are dedicated to fabrication, which is the act and process of manufacturing or inventing something. You could call it making something from scratch. Metal fabrication is the construction of metal items by means of cutting, bending, and assembling, and it's often taught at makerspaces. Because machines and their parts are almost always made of metal, future maintenance techs and engineers can benefit from these programs.

A key ingredient for any makerspace is usually experienced staff, who can teach how to use all the tools to build the items. While experts are great to teach others, John Spencer, who has written a few articles on makerspaces, said on Medium.com that teachers "don't have to know how to do everything in the makerspace." They can learn as they go along with the students, and they don't necessarily need the latest cutting edge equipment. Spencer joined forces with a teacher and together they learned Linux, hacked old computers, and got them working again. This was knowledge they could now share with students. As Spencer points out, limitations can be opportunities to innovate.

Machine maintenance can involve a lot of metalwork. Welding is an essential metalwork skill that uses tools to heat metals so they can be joined together, as well as cut or shaped.

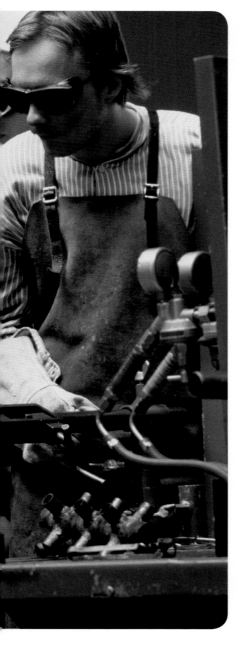

MAKER SKILLS FOR MACHINE MAINTENANCE

The "High School Makerspace Tools and Materials" guide features a section on metalworking, and it lists items needed to learn about welding (joining metals together through heat), brazing (a high-temperature metal-joining process using a filler, like a copper-zinc alloy, to connect the pieces), and soldering (a low-temperature metal-joining process using a filler often made from percentages of copper, tin, and silver). Soldering and material called soldering wire are often used to join electrical components.

Tools used for typical metalwork include arc welders, hand torches, band saws, clamps, pliers, drills, files, hammers, grinders, and grinding wheels.

AN INTRODUCTION TO ELECTRONICS

Machines may be made of metal, but it's their electronic components that make them function. Makerspaces are terrific training grounds to learn basic electronics. People know that electricity comes out of the wall socket or from batteries, but makerspaces teach how electrons flow through circuits to power our lights, televisions, stereos, computers, phones, and appliances. A circuit is a loop or pathway that electrons flow through. A light bulb can provide a simple example—when two wires are attached to a bulb, electrons can travel to and away from it in a circuit and light the bulb.

However, circuits are usually a much more complicated system of resistors, transistors, capacitors, inductors, and diodes, connected by wires—all components that perform different functions. Gradually, students master the language of electricity. For example, voltage is a measure of electrical potential designated in volts. Current is the amount of charge flowing through the circuit measured in amperes. Resistance is opposition to electrical current measured in ohms.

MAKING ELECTRONICS? GET ME A BREADBOARD

Makerspace projects often use a solderless breadboard for testing out or building circuitry. Why are they called breadboards? In days of old, when people wanted to experiment with electronics, they would grab the kitchen breadboard and use that as a platform to construct a rudimentary circuit with some nails, wire, and other components.

Among the common tools for electronics work are:

- A multimeter/oscilloscope to check voltages and continuity. Continuity shows if an electrical circuit is completely connected and able to conduct current.
- Flush/diagonal cutters for cutting wires and component leads or other wires.
- Wire strippers for removing the insulation from the tip of a wire so the wire can be connected to a component.
- A soldering iron for connecting wires and components to a circuit board.

For some, learning electronics may seem intimidating at first. But as the makerspace guide on StudyLib.com says, "it takes around 10 minutes to learn to solder, an hour to become proficient at using an oscilloscope, and about 15 minutes to master the rest of the tools."

CONNECTING TO THE COMPUTER UNIVERSE

Once a young maker understands some simple electronics, it's easier to grasp how computers operate as well. Many machines rely on computer components, and those who maintain them may be responsible for replacing or fixing computer parts that malfunction.

Nick Provenzano, a makerspace expert, uses various kits to teach students about computers and coding. Through Kano kits, young learners make a computer, learn some coding, and use different apps on the system they create. Makers often turn to small computers called microcontrollers to operate small devices. Popular maker-space microcontrollers are Arduino and Raspberry Pi. Using simple-to-program software, makers can make gizmos light up, move, and perform all sorts of functions. Makers like to share, and they often provide their code online in "libraries" for the world to see and use.

Microcontrollers can also work together with motors to perform advanced functions. Servomotors are often used because they are tiny and can work off of a 9-volt battery.

In this high-tech age, machine maintenance workers can benefit from learning computer repair. Here a young man wearing safety goggles fixes a broken element with a soldering tool.

Typically, robots run on motors, and with a pro-grammed microcontroller inside, a robot can come to life with movement, sounds, and lights. Robotics brings many of the maker elements together at once—metalwork, elec-tronics, and computers. Robotics projects can really lay the foundation for understanding the machines that many industries rely on. Makers have constructed soda-serving robots, floor-cleaning robots, and plant-watering robots, to name a few.

3D PRINTERS AND LASER CUTTERS

Besides using minicomputers, makers commonly design and create programs on standard laptops. Software such as Blender, Sketchup, Tinkercad, and 123D are used for cre-ating objects via 3D printers, with which many makerspaces are now equipped. By squeezing out thin layers of plastic, one on top of the other, these printers can churn out almost anything. Search online and you will see all sorts of items with 3D parts—unicycles, electric guitars, prosthetic limbs, small automobiles, and lawnmowers.

California's Contour Crafting even makes 3D-printed buildings. For those in machine maintenance, the printers can be a way to whip up an instant part. The knob breaks. The sprocket cracks. A 3D printer may be able to generate a sturdy replacement. These printers come in all sizes now-adays and they have dropped in cost—Staples sells a small machine for under $300.

A laser cutter is another more sophisticated machine found in some makerspaces. They use laser beams to cut complex shapes quickly and accurately from flat materials such as paper, wood, acrylic, cardboard, and felt. Then makers assemble these flat cutouts to create 3D structures. Craftspeople have used the machine to produce clocks, coasters, candleholders, and beyond. Or laser cutters can be used for etching—a person could etch their name into an iPod case or a name on a dog tag. One project online shows how young makers used a laser cutter to make the character Pickle Rick from *Rick and Morty*.

Another "cutting-edge" technology employed by makers is CNC machining. CNC means computer numerical control, and CNC machines are programmed with software to precisely cut materials of all kinds including steel,

Laser cutting machines are used to make high quality parts for other machines. Pictured, a laser cutter slices through a stainless steel plate.

aluminum, and wood in three dimensions. CNC routers are designed to cut softer material like wood, plastic, and sometimes metal. These machines can carve a piece of wood into a cabinet door, for example. CNC mills are machines designed to cut metal and can transform a block of steel into engine components. Computer-aided design and computer-aided manufacturing software tells the CNC machines exactly what to do. A computer program directs motors and drives in their movement. CAMaster.com says that the spindle is the part of the machine responsible for cutting, and it rotates at different speeds depending on what is being cut. The StudyLib makerspace guide says that it differs from laser cutting in two ways: it carves two or three dimensionally and carves a wider range of materials and thicker materials.

CHAPTER TWO

"MAKING" YOUR WAY TO A SUCCESSFUL CAREER

Makerspaces can introduce you to the skills needed for machine maintenance and give experience by working on real projects. On Medium.com, John Spencer wrote that the maker mindset prepares you to solve problems and try new things. Makers become innovators. So someone who enters the field of machine maintenance may rise in the job ranks by coming up with new and more efficient methods of doing things.

Spencer tells how the makerspace mindset led one student from learning to code in the sixth grade to going on in life to earn a master's degree in engineering.

College of the Canyons in Santa Clarita, California, maintains its own makerspace and FabLab (a small-scale workshop for fabrication projects). At an event hosted at the college promoting careers in manufacturing and advanced technologies, local high school senior and engineering student Niamani Knight said, "With over 200,000 jobs

Machine maintenance technicians may apply their skills in their office buildings keeping elements such as heat and air conditioning units and elevators repaired and operating correctly.

available in the manufacturing industry, students should know this is a booming career option."

THE BASICS OF MACHINE MAINTENANCE

Because makerspaces guide students from conceiving an idea to manufacturing a product, they have been ideal training grounds for entering the manufacturing field— one that depends on machine maintenance professionals.

Machinery maintenance workers perform regular upkeep and repairs, and they apply their know-how to machines like conveyor belts or packaging equipment.

A lot of products we see around us every day depend on the machine maintenance worker. For example, those paper towels in the kitchen may have resulted from the labors of Jennifer K., a machine technician at Bedford Paper in Wisconsin. She's responsible for maintaining a variety of machines related to paper products. When it comes to making paper towels, manufacturers continually strive to improve absorbency. Embossing and laminating are two processes that do just that. Most towels have an embossed pattern made up of protrusions, and this embossing is used to increase bulk, absorbency, softness, and roll size. One apparatus that Jennifer maintains is a rewinding machine. Search for paper towel or toilet paper rewinding machines online to view these machines in action as they spool paper products and cut them to desired dimensions.

MAINTENANCE TECHS WEAR MANY HATS

A machine maintenance career doesn't necessarily focus on one type of machine, and in fact, many maintenance technicians are jacks-of-all-trades. Sometimes maintenance technicians work for buildings and properties, responsible for all the major mechanical elements from lighting to elevators to refrigeration to air-conditioning and heating. They can work at hospitals, schools, hotels, department stores, and offices.

When electrical switches, outlets, and circuit break-ers fail, the maintenance tech can fix them. This can take patience, trying multiple possible solutions before hitting on what might get things up and operating again.

You've heard the expression that something can run like a well-oiled machine. Keeping mechanical parts cleaned and lubricated is a major part of the job. Technicians depend on their tools to take care of business, and they have to have good dexterity with their hands. These tools can be standard screwdrivers, wrenches, hammers, pliers, tape measures, and wire cutters. If something jams, a wire

Elevator technicians have an important job, keeping people safe as they use elevators in tall buildings. They also install elevators, as this tech demonstrates.

frays, or a moving part starts to wobble, a maintenance tech can rush to the rescue. They use a variety of power tools, including drills and saws.

They keep a careful eye on monitors, which can warn if a system is getting overheated or if certain element is low (fuel, paper, ink, etc.). When warnings appear, the technician may swing into action correcting any problems.

Sometimes these workers will be the muscle power behind initially setting up equipment and taking it down when an operation has to be dismantled. They may have to put their backs into lifting with hoists or winches, or possibly using tractors, cranes, or forklifts.

Because it can be physical work with heavy equipment, the job can be more dangerous than others. These laborers are more apt to suffer cuts, bruises, electrical shocks, and other injuries. A lot of the same precautions taken in a makerspace apply here. Employees wear the right protective gear for the job—gloves, hardhats, earplugs, goggles, heavy boots, etc. Be warned that careers related to machine work tend to have higher injury rights than the average job.

Technicians generally enjoy the physical aspect of the job but the tasks demand stamina. Technicians may climb ladders, crawl into tight spaces, and unload supplies. Some work areas can be stifling hot while others may be freezing.

The hours are often regular, but technicians have to be ready to jump to action when there is an emergency and, in some cases, when machines operate around the clock, they may be required to work overnight shifts.

Technicians benefit from certain soft skills as well. They have to be good communicators as they consult with managers and employers about the work that needs to be done.

They also keep careful logs of their work—a valuable reference when future work is required. Because some tasks may be beyond their talents, technicians need to know when to call in specialists—heating and air-conditioning pros, carpenters, electricians, plumbers, etc.

One maintenance technician on an internet forum said, "I enjoy making and keeping things working and the variety of work manufacturing parts, repairing parts, and the challenge of learning a piece of equipment to troubleshoot skillfully."

HANDS-ON AND CLASSROOM INSTRUCTION

A technician can usually get started in a job with a high school diploma. While in high school, classes in math, physics, and chemistry can be helpful. To advance on the job additional education is required. Those interested in this type of work may pursue a two- or four-year apprenticeship program at a community college or tech school. The US Department of Labor has called apprenticeships the workforce solution for the advanced manufacturing industry. Apprenticeships combine on-the-job learning with related in-class instruction.

The US Labor Department tells how the Rolls-Royce company needed more workers to help operate its CNC machines and to keep up with the demand for its automobiles. The firm also developed apprenticeships for its precision aircraft part production. The company turned to Virginia's Community College Workforce Alliance and local high schools to figure out a way to train young people for a future career. The students trained at the community college, and Rolls-Royce chipped in funds to pay for the tuition of first-year apprentices. That could be an amount in excess

Apprenticeships give students the chance to learn in the classroom and while getting hands-on training on the job, often earning a paycheck for their work hours.

of $7,000. Some of the company's apprenticeship programs even pay you while you are learning.

When it comes to aircraft components, production requires very precisely fine-tuned equipment, so training is very specific. One of the jobs, for example, requires using a fiber-optic camera to look for microscopic defects in turbine blades.

This apprenticeship, like many others, takes about three years to complete with the mix of on-the-job training and classroom work. The American Institute for Innovative Apprenticeship (AIIA) lists the apprenticeship for industrial maintenance repairer as taking four years. These apprentices are paid wages on an increasingly progressive schedule.

Apprenticeships also give trainees some universal work skills such as leadership, customer service, communication, and proper workplace appearance. Once an apprentice completes his or her training, he or she advances to become a journeyman. (In Canada, the title has changed to journeyperson to recognize that it applies to all genders.) At this stage, the worker is recognized as qualified and skilled in his or her particular trade, a level of experience and training that employers look for in their hires.

APPRENTICE SKILLS FOR MAINTENANCE REPAIR

The AIIA lists the following skills that an industrial maintenance repairer should learn in an apprenticeship:

1. Basic reading skills
2. Good time management skills (i.e., efficient use of time on job site)
3. Lay out and plan pump installation
4. Kinetic energy terminology
5. Reading measuring devices
6. Reading and interpreting drawings
7. Reading and interpreting catalog and rough-in information
8. Reading and interpreting specifications
9. Preparing a bill of materials
10. Reading and interpreting applicable codes
11. Identifying basic structural framing components
12. Performing general mathematical calculations
13. Creating engineering drawings and related documents for design using computer-assisted programs

The Institute also lists some more specific mechanical skills that are taught:

1. Reading blueprints, specifications, and sketches using basic mathematics
2. Setting up and operating various kinds of machine such as lathes, planers, and milling machines
3. Performing simple layout work and making templates
4. Using various power tools
5. Using precision measuring instruments such as height and depth gauges, calipers, and micrometers
6. Acquiring a broad knowledge of mechanical principles

SPECIALIZING TO ADVANCE

Maintenance technicians looking to advance can earn a journeyman card in a number of areas, including iron-work, millwright, or pipefitter. Two common skill areas that a maintenance tech may want to develop are in plumbing and electricity. Plumbers and plumbing technicians repair piping fixtures and appliances in connection with the water supply and drainage systems inside and outside of build-ings. Electricians install, maintain, and repair electrical power, communications, lighting, and control systems in homes, businesses, and factories, according to the BLS. People enter both these professions through apprentice-ship programs.

CLIMBING THE CAREER LADDER

Career titles often have some overlap when it comes to responsibilities. In general, industrial machinery mechan-ics (also called maintenance machinists) may have more responsibilities than technicians. These mechanics may handle more of the repairs compared to the technicians, and they work with all sorts of devices from hydraulic lifts to automobile assembly line conveyor belts to robotic welding arms. Collegegrad.com says that these professionals refer to technical manuals to pinpoint a machine problem.

An example that Collegegrad.com gives is a machine that has an irregular vibration. The mechanic must evalu-ate if the shaking is coming from worn belts, weak motor bearings, or some other issue. Computerized diagnostic systems may help pinpoint the source of problems. Once the trouble source is detected, the machinery mechanic may dismantle the equipment to repair or replace parts. After the fix is made, mechanics test the gear to ensure that everything is working correctly.

WORKING AS A MILLWRIGHT

Some view millwrights as a type of maintenance technician while others call them industrial mechanics. Many employment sites post listings specifically seeking millwright maintenance technicians. Originally, millwrights constructed only mills—whether they be for flour, wood, paper, or another product.

Today, millwrights set up, service, and take down all types of industrial machines. The job requires a high level of meticulousness. When these pros dismantle a machine, they carefully label and store every part in case the equipment is to be set up at a new location. They often have a broad base of knowledge on a variety of machines. They braze, weld, cut, and use a variety of precise measuring tools from levels to micrometers, an instrument with a spindle moved by a finely threaded screw, for the measurement of thicknesses and short lengths.

On the Hammer9 Union Carpenters and Millwrights website, apprentice Marcus Moss writes, "I love being a millwright. I like layout

and precision work the best. But you do different things every day. And the instructors have taught me a lot. Every job I've been on, everybody's got each other's back. It really is a brotherhood."

Ashley Holder works on various machines as a millwright at Robins Airforce Base in Georgia. Here he slides metal guardrail tubing onto a saw.

ADVANCING TO BECOME AN ENGINEER

While technicians work mostly on maintaining and repair, engineers are the actual makers. An electrical engineer takes a step beyond electrician to create the products and systems that operate on electricity. A mechanical engineer takes a step beyond maintenance to develop and modify machines using principles of mechanical theory.

Mechanics has been called the study of motion of matter and the forces that cause such motion. It involves many of the principles taught in physics classes—understanding the aspects of matter and energy, and subject matter such as light, heat, force, motion, sound, electricity, and magnetism. Some of the advanced concepts mechanical engineers may apply in their work are thermodynamics, kinematics, fluid dynamics, and heat transfer. The handiwork of mechanical engineers touches almost everything around us. They work in the automotive, aerospace, electronics, biotechnology, and energy industries.

Top employers of mechanical engineers and technicians include automobile parts manufacturing and architectural, engineering, and research industries.

If something has moving parts, a mechanical engineer's ingenuity is behind it. These engineers design, develop, build, and test mechanical equipment. The Bureau of Labor Statistics gives a broad range of how diverse their work can be. They may design electric generators, internal combustion engines, and steam and gas turbines. They may create refrigeration and air-conditioning systems. Mechanical engineers are behind elevators and escalators, conveyor belts, robotics, and automated machinery.

Computer know-how is a vital part of their work. Machinery often runs on computer components, and testing, simulating, and analyzing results requires computer power. Students wanting to pursue a career in mechanical engineering can earn a two- or four-year degree in mechanical engineering or mechanical engineering technology. Some colleges and universities offer even more advanced programs to earn a bachelor's and a master's degree in mechanical engineering in five or six years. Those looking to climb higher on the career ladder can earn different certifications, such as a professional engineering (PE) license.

In addition to taking advantage of makerspace courses, a high school student may get a jump on engineering education by attending an engineering summer camp. Find out more at the Engineering Education Service Center website, which has a page dedicated to these camps.

A CAREER EXPECTED TO GROW

The Bureau of Labor Statistics predicts that general maintenance and repair workers may expect 8 percent employment growth between 2016 and 2026. The same growth rate goes for other maintenance, repair, and installation occupations, as well as engineers. Opportunities for mechanical engineers are expected to be just slightly higher. Those with training in the latest software tools, particularly for computational design and simulation should find many job prospects on the horizon, according to the BLS.

The median annual wage for general maintenance and repair workers was $37,670 in May 2017, according to the BLS, and for those in manufacturing salaries averaged $44,260. Because mechanical engineers have significantly more training than technicians, they earn significantly more as well with annual median salary in May 2017 of more than $85,000. Some earn as much as $134,000 per year. Salaries and wages change frequently, though, so keeping the current average on hand is smart as you begin looking for a job.

CHAPTER THREE

MAKING PRODUCTS IN FACTORIES: ASSEMBLY LINE WORK

Machine mechanics work in manufacturing keeping the wheels of American industry spinning. Assembly line machines churn out and package all types of products from food to toys to clothing. The equipment that handles it all has to be serviced and repaired; sometimes it has to be installed or dismantled. The need for new employees entering this field is great.

In an interview in *Popular Mechanics*, a representative from Airstream trailers said, "Younger folks in the US are not really targeting manufacturing as a career. That's a challenge, just trying to make sure the younger generations are as good as the older generations at building things, because we're such a handcrafted product."

When the accounting organization Deloitte issued its report on the skills gap in US manufacturing from 2015 to 2025, the company found that manufacturers were reporting drastically lacking the talent they need to keep their businesses growing. They found that the need for skilled workers is expected to explode over the next decades as 3.5 million manufacturing jobs will need to be filled, but they expect 2 million jobs to go unfulfilled because of a skills gap. The majority of executives polled for the survey said that current employees do not have sufficient skills in computers, technical training, problem solving, and math.

MAKERSPACES MAKE MANUFACTURING COOL

Makerspaces have also helped make manufacturing jobs cooler because the whole movement in general has a

DOES MANUFACTURING HAVE AN IMAGE PROBLEM?

Pia Kumar, the head of corporate development with Universal Plastics, wrote on the business site Axial.net that she thinks manufacturing has an image problem. She wrote: "Old stereotypes of backbreaking labor and grimy working conditions still dominate the minds of younger candidates. The world has given celebrity status to high technology and cutting edge entrepreneurship, making traditional 'old economy' industries, such as manufacturing, seem comparatively unsexy."

She believes that young people may not be seeing the exciting technology behind many manufacturing jobs. Factory workers today may be cutting steel with water jets, lasers, or plasma cutters. Or they may be programming robots to paint and package products.

more modern slant. Gene Sherman, a self-described maker who has been a machinist and toolmaker, is now an educator and entrepreneur as the founder of Vocademy—The Makerspace in Riverside, California. He believes that the next generation of skilled and motivated manufacturers is coming directly from the maker movement.

These workers on the assembly line at the Tesla car factory in Fremont, California, demonstrate manufacturing and machine technician skills in action.

In an interview with Michael C. Anderson in *Manufacturing Engineering* magazine, Sherman said the problem with makerspaces is that they are like twenty-four-hour gyms—students often just stop in when they can so they often just develop skills to a hobbyist level. Sherman has tried to shape his makerspace into a more practical training ground. For example, students can take a specific three-hour class in how to operate a milling machine. A milling machine, basically a rotating cutter, is used to make complex shapes from metal (and sometimes wood or plastic). Milling is used to produce parts for automobiles, telecommunications, and electronics.

KEEP THOSE MOTORS RUNNING

Machine maintenance technicians often work on engines, whether they are for transportation or powering any number of industrial plants. Engine expertise is needed in the automotive industry, aviation, and marine maintenance. These specialists may work on diesel engine generators used by state-of-the-art hospitals, manufacturing plants, public utilities, telecommunication organizations, mining, and many other operations.

One type of machine maintenance that most people are familiar with is for car engines. Drive through any town in America, and you'll find automotive shops where mechanics and technicians keep engines humming. Also called service technicians or service techs, these skilled workers inspect, maintain, and repair cars and light trucks.

Engines both large and small need maintenance from time to time. This technician works to repair an airplane engine.

CAR MAINTENANCE IN THE MODERN WORLD

These workers repair engines, transmissions, and drive belts. Increasingly, they have to master the electronic and computerized components that are taking over newer cars, such as screens that provide a view when backing

THE AUTOMOTIVE TECHNICIAN CHECKLIST

The Bureau of Labor Statistics published this list of duties that are performed specifically by automotive technicians:

- **Identify problems by using computerized diagnostic equipment**
- **Plan work procedures using charts, technical manuals, and experience**
- **Test parts and systems to ensure that they work properly**
- **Follow checklists to ensure that all critical parts are examined**
- **Perform basic care and maintenance, including changing oil, checking fluid levels, and rotating tires**
- **Repair or replace worn parts, such as brake pads, wheel bearings, and sensors**
- **Perform repairs to manufacturer and customer specifications**
- **Explain automotive problems and repairs to clients**

up, speakerphone capabilities through the car radio via Bluetooth, lane departure warnings, automatic emergency brake sensors, and USB ports. Today's mechanics and techs may perform computer diagnosis on a vehicle. Since 1996, all vehicles are equipped with a standard plug, called the on-board diagnostics, or O.B.D.-II port, to access a car's emissions codes. With the right computer plug-ins, mechanics can read a whole range of diagnostic codes. Maybe the engine cooler sensor is broken and unable to report the correct temperature.

These technicians, like other maintenance techs, rely on many standard tools—wrenches, screwdrivers, welding torches, and others. Technicians may specialize in specific components, such as air-conditioning systems, brakes, front end, or transmission.

Diesel service technicians do similar work, but only on the big diesel engines that power buses and trucks.

EDUCATION DRIVES TECHNICIANS FORWARD

Education to become an auto tech can start with a high school course. Check out the website for the Automotive Youth Educational Systems (AYES).

This national organization describes itself as a partnership of automobile manufacturers and dealers and education departments in many states around the

Many schools offer auto mechanic training. Trainees can earn official certification.

country. More than 4,500 car dealerships participate in these programs that train young workers and get them jobs.

Students often hone their skills in a one- or two-year associate's degree program in automotive repair or technology offered at community colleges and technical schools.

Automotive Service Excellence programs, lasting six to twelve months, give workers credentials, demonstrating that they have achieved industry-standard skills. Mechanics can earn credentials showing that they have mastered automotive transmissions, heating and air-conditioning, manual drive train, suspension and steering, brakes, electrical and electronic systems, engine performance, and performance repair. Each of these categories requires two years experience before a worker can jump ahead and take the test.

THE JOYS OF AUTO TECH WORK

In an article on his website, automotive technician Jesse Adams says that he finds the job rewarding from disassembly, reassembly, diagnosing problems, and helping people. He says he loves working with the tools and solving the issues that are affecting the cars: "When you top it off by returning what you've diagnosed and repaired to the person who owns it and is ecstatic that their baby has been fixed, it makes you feel kind of like Superman."

Employment of automotive service technicians and mechanics is projected to grow 6 percent from 2016 to 2026, according to the Bureau of Labor Statistics.

BY AIR, BY SEA, BY RAILROAD

Machine maintenance for transportation goes beyond road vehicles. Airports, marinas, and train yards also need technicians for their unique machinery. The duties are similar to auto mechanics, but the equipment is distinct.

For example, jet engines and car engines are fundamentally different—a car engine combusts air and gasoline to produce pressurized exhaust gasses that push against pistons, which make wheels turn. A jet engine combusts air and kerosene and pushes all of its exhaust gasses out the back to propel the airplane forward. While airplanes may be the primary type of aircraft a technician services, they also fix and maintain helicopters and planes that are specifically designed for crop dusting. In addition to commercial airports, they may labor with the military and agricultural businesses. Overall employment of aircraft and avionics equipment mechanics and technicians is projected to grow 5 percent from 2016 to 2026, according to the Bureau of Labor Statistics. Motorboat mechanics have their own unique skill for engine maintenance. A boat engine is different in that it is designed to perform in rugged conditions presented by salt and water. Generally, a marine engine is more powerful, needing to move a heavier load than a car.

Today's trains usually operate using a diesel engine that drives either an electrical DC or AC engine.

THE MAKERSPACE ENGINE CONNECTION

Some makerspaces may guide young participants in the process of making an engine, and also offer simple projects to help makers understand how motors work. Makerspaces .com gives instructions on how to construct a mini electric car using a DC motor, AA batteries, and a switch. The words *motor* and *engine* often mean the same thing, as they both supply motive power for a vehicle or for some other device with moving parts.

THE MOTORS OF INDUSTRY

When it comes to turning the wheels of industry, commercial enterprises rely on all sorts of motors, such as DC series motors, DC shunt motors, slip ring induction motors, and repulsion motors. Different industrial automation situations require different types of motors.

The AC induction motor is the dominant motor technology in use today and has long been the industry workhorse. These are commonly used for pumps, blowers, conveyors, and other industrial machinery. Conveyors are a type of material-handling equipment that assists in moving products, packages, food, or equipment from one place inside a facility to another or through various stages of automated manufacturing or finishing. The Industrial Quick Search Manufacturer Directory explains that conveyors, which are usually motorized, move a broad range of items; different conveyor configurations are available to meet

Induction motors, like this one, are often used in industry. They are known for their simple design, durable construction, and relative ease to maintain.

the material-handling needs of manufacturers and distributors everywhere. According to conveyor-systems.biz, belt conveyors are the most common, followed by chain conveyors, roller conveyors, spiral conveyors, overhead conveyors, and conveyor systems, which may use combinations of many different conveyor types. Conveyors are usually motorized.

Search online and you'll find scores of companies seeking conveyor maintenance technicians. For example, Cardinal Glass Industries in Buckeye, Arizona, was looking to hire a qualified electro-mechanical technician who could ensure the operation of its machinery and mechanical equipment by completing preventive maintenance requirements on motors, pneumatics, conveyor systems, and production machines; following diagrams, sketches, operations manuals, manufacturer's instructions, and engineering specifications; and troubleshooting malfunctions.

In addition to manufacturers, engines may be humming along at large hospitals, telecommunications organizations, and mining operations, to name a few.

CHAPTER FIVE

HIGH-TECH MAINTENANCE

Technological advances have paved the way for a whole new type of sophisticated machine mainte-nance. In a high-tech world, a maintenance pro may need expertise in computers, complex instrumentation, and digital cameras.

CHURNING OUT THE CHIPS

Chip making is one of the jobs at the heart of the tech industry. This vital computer component starts with something very sim-ple—sand or, more specifically, silica sand. Silicon is the most plentiful ingredient on Earth except for oxygen. Chips are also called integrated circuits or semiconductors.

The silicon chip has an integrated circuit embedded in it. That chip can hold millions of transistors and elec-tronic components. The transistors act as on/off switches, controlling the flow of electricity and processing information. Intel, one of the world's leading manufacturers of chips, says that chips are some of the most complex devices ever manufactured. The manufacturing process

The skills developed building and creating with electronics in a makerspace can apply in a real-work setting. Here, a worker assembles electronic components.

takes hundreds of steps, and while the end-resulting chip may look flat, it is made up of as many as thirty layers of complex circuitry. Without these chips, we'd have no smartphones, no laptop computers, tablets, and no satellite communication. The chips are embedded in all sorts of gadgets and in automobiles.

KEEPING IT CLEAN

The manufacturing technicians who help churn out these chips work in ultraclean environments aptly called clean rooms. As Intel says on their website, these are thousands of times cleaner than hospital operating rooms. These tech workers put on hairnets and all-white uniforms called bunny suits, which feature hoods, shoe covers, and two pairs of gloves to help protect the chips from any contaminants, such as hair, bacteria, and lint. They also don safety goggles, in part for their own protection, but mostly again to protect the chips. The technicians have to be ultraclean—they carefully wash their hands and face. They wear no makeup or perfume. When the work shift starts, they have to make sure they've used the restroom because they are usually required to work a shift without a break. A Bloomberg News article titled "How

Intel Makes a Chip" describes how they write notes in the clean room using sterile pens and paper.

THE CHIP-MAKING PROCESS

Intel describes the process very well on their website—a photolithographic printing process forms a chip's multilayered transistors and interconnects (electrical circuits) on a wafer. When the layers are set, a computer performs the wafer sort test, which evaluates if the chip will perform up to standard. The company details how the wafer is cut into individual pieces called die. The die is packaged between a substrate and a heat spreader to form a completed processor. The package protects the die and delivers critical power and electrical connections when placed directly into a computer circuit board or mobile device, such as a smartphone or tablet.

To get this job done, manufacturing technicians operate, maintain, and repair the specialized processing equipment. In addition to this attentive hands-on work, these professionals collect and check data and perform tests to debug equipment.

Entering the career takes a two- to four-year technical degree related to electronic engineering technology.

On the website AnandTech, one seasoned professional in the field says, "I am an engineering technician at Intel, and spend the majority of my work life in the fab [short for fabrication center]. And I absolutely love it. My job is spent either performing repairs/ maintenance on the semiconductor manufacturing equipment, or running experiments to improve the process."

He warns that the position can be potentially dangerous with "lots of high voltage, fast moving robots, and nasty chemicals," but everything is well regulated so that conditions are relatively safe.

Machine maintenance technicians with a passion for the latest technology may find an opportunity producing computer components like this circuit board.

MAINTAINING THE SMART MACHINES

Computer maintenance overall is a field that needs qualified employees. Positions may include building, testing, troubleshooting, installing, configuring, and packaging material. Look at the computers in your life, and you'll know that a professional was behind them, playing a role in the construction of mainframes, servers, personal computers, workstations, and laptops. Companies such as Apple, Dell Technologies, Hewlett Packard Enterprise (HP), and IBM all need machine technicians on the production end.

While some computer technicians may be working behind the scenes on the manufacturing end of computers, others are troubleshooting and resolving computer problems with customers who own computers. A computer technician finds employment in all different businesses and industries making sure their computer systems are up and running smoothly in offices, hospitals, universities, corporations, and other organizations. Without these technicians, operations shut down and can lose money fast. Makerspaces may

Today's world runs on computer technology, so the more you know about computers, the better. Some makerspace classes not only teach how to repair computers but also how to code.

give attendees training on how to fix computers, and something that was at first a personal passion can turn into a full-time career.

The Bureau of Labor Statistics predicts that tech jobs will grow faster than average for all jobs at a rate of 13 percent this decade, but it's not just hiring demand that makes this industry one to watch. *US News & World Report*'s Best Technology Jobs of 2018 says that these positions are high-paying jobs that boast low unemployment rates.

A computer technician on CareerCast writes:

> I get paid for my hobby. A man who loves what he does doesn't work a day in his life. I feel like this is what I was meant to do. I was fortunate in that I was able to move a hobby into a profession via training. I got started by being a hobbyist and spending more and more time at the computer store. One day the owner asked if I wanted to work there. I did and got more and more experience and the owner paid for my training. The only thing I would change is I'd have gone to college for it straight from high school instead of waiting.

Like a lot of careers that can rise from the makerspace experience, a computer technician gains hands-on-experience using different tools to repair the components—screwdrivers, tweezers, needle-nosed pliers, wire cutters, and chip extractors. Computer techs may take computer-programming classes in high school and in college. While there is no industry standard, high school graduates might consider taking six- to twelve-month certificate and one- to two-year associate's degree programs offered by junior colleges, technical institutes, and vocational schools, according to the BLS. Passing the Computer Technology Industry Association's (CompTIA) A+ certification exam shows that an individual has competency in a number of areas, such as computer networks, servers, and security applications. Employment for computer support specialists is expected to grow by 11 percent from 2016 to 2026.

SEND IN THE ROBOTS

Makerspaces provide a terrific pathway for learning robotics. As the Makerspace for Education website says, "Robotics are machines that can do three things: sense, act, and think." Some makerspaces use a program through SONY called Koov that lets students build robots with sensors, lights, motors, and a programmable microcontroller. Makerspaces.com shows a number of nifty robotics projects, including a cardboard hydraulic arm that can lift up a can of Coke or a cardboard frog robot.

Like other maintenance techs, robotics technicians build, maintain, test, and repair robotics, often as they relate to automated production systems. They have to have a firm grasp on electronics, computers, and hardware to construct complex precision machinery. They can be like master puzzle builders putting together complicated and detailed drawings, specifications, sketches, bills of materials, production orders, and instructions. They're not only puzzle builders, they also often make the pieces for the puzzle—using welding equipment to cut or weld parts and operate lathes, mills, and grinders to machine or fabricate parts needed to build the systems. They

The Institute of Electrical and Electronics Engineers lists robotics engineer as one of the hottest careers. Makerspaces often help young people build their own simple robots.

usually have a broad knowledge of hydraulics and pneumatics (both technologies use a fluid [liquid or gas] to transmit power from one location to another).

Some techs work on surgical robotics, which are being used to perform operations in hospitals. Techs at Google are working on human automatons and driverless cars. In 2012, Rethink Robotics debuted Baxter, a humanoid robot with a touchscreen face and two arms that could learn repetitive tasks quickly.

The Bureau of Labor Statistics suggests earning at least a two-year degree or postsecondary certificate at a vocational–technical school or community colleges. Coursework may include study in electromechanics, industrial maintenance, and process control (using industrial systems to achieve a production level that is consistent, economic, and safe.) As a type of electromechanical technician, a robotics pro is expected to see growth in job opportunities of 4 percent from 2016 to 2026.

CHAPTER SIX

MAINTAINING THE HOME AND OFFICE

Many machines require maintenance and repair on a smaller level, in the home or office.

Just look around your own home and you'll see opportunities for a technician. They service all sorts of washing machines, dryers, dishwashers, refrigerators, freezers, televisions, and air-conditioning units. The job is simple—when an appliance breaks, they are called in to fix it.

Sometimes an appliance technician will run his or her own repair shop as well, where customers can drop off small items to be fixed. Wherever they work, appliance technicians are constantly on the go, traveling to different homes or offices and often having to maneuver their bodies into tight spaces. They may be lying on their backs to fix wiring or crouching in crawl spaces to examine a furnace.

Sometimes machine maintenance technicians apply their trade in the home or office. They may fix all sorts of equipment, from copiers to washing machines to refrigerators (as pictured here).

THE OFFICE MACHINES: THE ELEVATOR

Offices have a vast range of machines to keep up and operating, from the copy machine to the elevators. Office workers may ride the elevator every day, but they probably don't think at all about the technicians who keep the apparatus functioning properly. In a sense, though, their lives are in the hands of an elevator repairperson. If there's a malfunction in the elevator, it can bring disaster.

HONING FIX-IT SKILLS AT MAKERSPACES AND REPAIR CAFÉS

Makerspaces are the perfect environments to sharpen these kinds of fix-it skills. Several movements have started to encourage people to get in the habit of repairing things, rather than throwing them away. Several makerspaces advertise Fix-it Fridays that encourage tinkerers of all ages to gather to fix broken irons, cell phones, radios, DVD players, toasters, coffee machines, bicycles, sewing machines, vacuum cleaners, and many other gadgets. Fixers believe you can save money and stop unnecessary waste by learning to mend items rather than toss them. While some fixers meet up at official makerspaces, others are connecting under the umbrella of the name Repair Café. The Repair Café Facebook page provides information on the community of local groups in the United States that are organizing their own Repair Café meetings. Public and school libraries have jumped on board the movement as well. An article in *American Libraries* magazine describes how a middle school student brought her broken electric scooter into a public library in Boulder, Colorado, that held a U-Fix-It Clinic in its makerspace. Working together with the clinic coordinator, she made the repair and was soon zipping around the parking lot. She was so inspired by her success that she returned again to the clinic and told the leader she intended to become an engineer. Another eight-year-old learned to fix a broken lamp, and it became her mission to help everyone with a broken lamp. Certainly, if appliance repair appeals as a career, this is a great place to start.

On a minor level, if the elevator is out of order, workers must take the dreaded stairs. Accurate and regular maintenance is essential to assure that the elevator can perform its hundreds of trips per day.

In an article on The Art of Manliness website, an elevator mechanic, Casey Planchon, talks about the ups and downs of the career. He had served in the army and was looking for a job where he could be active and use his hands. He entered an apprenticeship program with a local elevator union. He works on two types of elevators—traction and hydraulic. Traction, the most common type of elevator, functions on a system of electric motors that pull

As long as there are tall buildings, the world will need elevator maintenance technicians. In fact, opportunities are expected to grow faster than the average for all jobs.

rolling steel ropes over deeply grooved pulleys, typically called sheaves in the elevator biz.

Planchon also works on hydraulic elevators. They operate through a submersible motor, which is completely immersed in fluid—in this case, hydraulics fluid, which is either pumped into the jacks to lift the elevator or drained into a tank to lower it.

"The satisfaction of building and fixing elevators, escalators, and moving walkways are the best of all the trades," says Planchon in the article. Plus, he appreciates that elevator technician work pays very well.

He warns that the work is dirty, physical, and sometimes a bit dangerous—he can sometimes find himself several stories up an elevator shaft carrying heavy equipment.

To enter this type of career, the BLS recommends that high school students take classes in math, mechanical drawing, and shop, then go on to pursue an apprenticeship. Opportunities in this field are expected to be abundant, with the BLS projecting job growth at 12 percent from 2016 to 2026.

WORKING AS A HVAC TECHNICIAN

Another technician career of note that is in huge demand is as an HVAC technician. People want their living and work environments to be neither too hot nor too cold, and that's where the HVAC technician plays a vital role. HVAC means heating, ventilation, and air conditioning, and HVAC technicians maintain extensive systems that run throughout a building, or they may work on heating unit and air conditioning in homes. HVAC technicians may specialize in one area as well, such as refrigeration systems, but they often are asked to repair a range of heating units, ventilation systems, and air conditioners on a large scale. HVACclasses.org says that a property management company or a general contractor may employ these professionals, or they may work independently as small-business owners.

As with many technicians, these jobs are calm while things are working, but if a system breaks down they must jump into action to make the fix, which may occur at any time of day.

Dan Deardon, the owner of Just Right Air, runs his own HVAC service and has been in the business for decades, according to a profile on JustRightAir.com. On the website, he says: "I didn't really like school much…In my senior year, my dad said to me, 'You like doing things with your hands. You're very mechanical.' He knew I liked the outdoors," explains Deardon. Right out of high school, Deardon chose heating and air-conditioning repair as a career and hasn't looked back. "I went to technical college in HVAC and here I am."

Deardon goes on to say that he enjoys problem solving, not being stuck in an office, the variety of work at many different locations, and the grateful customers.

As with many trades, the real training for an HVAC takes place in an apprenticeship program, but while in high school, students are advised to bone up on their math, physics, and learn any electronics they can—again, the makerspace can be a perfect environment for that. Trainees often take HVAC classes at technical and trade schools or community colleges. The programs last about six months to two years, and students leave with an associate's degree or certificate.

This career is in high demand, offering more opportunities than many other fields, with employment projected to grow at 15 percent between 2016 and 2026—far faster than the average, according to the Bureau of Labor Statistics. Part of the reason for the surge in opportunity is a growing demand for energy efficiency and pollution reduction. Increasingly, HVAC technicians are called in to retrofit, upgrade, or entirely replace climate-control systems.

Once you have some training and have set your sights on a certain job, the next step is to start the wheels in motion to secure employment. At the top of the list—reach out to whom you know. In an interview with NPR, Matt Youngquist, the president of Career Horizons, says the successful job hunt is all about networking.

USE YOUR VAST NETWORK

"At least 70 percent, if not 80 percent, of jobs are not published," says Youngquist in the interview with NPR. "And yet most people—they are spending 70 or 80 percent of their time surfing the net versus getting out there, talking to employers, taking some chances [and] realizing that the vast majority of hiring is friends and acquaintances hiring other trusted friends and acquaintances."

To seriously find work, seekers have to treat the hunt like a nine-to-five job. Drop emails to friends, classmates,

Once a student has some training and skills, the next step is to go through the hiring process. This requires networking to find opportunities and completing a successful job interview.

family, and former coworkers telling them what type of job you're looking for. Check out companies where you might have a personal connection. The LinkedIn networking site is specifically designed for jobseekers. Users post profiles on the site, sharing their professional background and qualifications, and employers comb the profiles looking for the right talent. It's a good way to locate people you know who might be working at a company you like.

Through other social media sites like Facebook and Twitter, job seekers can broadcast to all their connections that they are looking for work. Spreading the word is the key to landing that perfect employment opportunity.

Many maintenance technicians pursue skilled trades, and a site like Tradecrews caters exclusively to them. As their site says, "TradeCrews is a platform that allows you to search for and connect with other users, find training opportunities, employment, apprenticeships, and view business profiles." The site is not only for students, graduates, and job seekers, but tradesmen and companies who want to directly hire them.

To take your networking game to another level, consider attending a job fair. Hundreds of employers and recruiters typically gather at these events. Search online and you'll find many options geared for maintenance workers such as the Central Ohio Facilities Maintenance Expo or the South Puget Sound Facilities Maintenance Expo.

Makerspaces can be a perfect setting to make job connections—meeting with other people with common interests and mentors who have many links to opportunities. An article on the Association of Equipment Manufacturers website told how manufacturers are tapping into talent at makerspaces. The Marmon Group, a company that holds shares in various industrial companies, in Chicago, for instance, forged a partnership with a Chicago business incubator and makerspace called mHub. Here they "found a different set of talent than they would have probably hired on their own."

APPLY FOR THE APPRENTICESHIP

The beauty of apprenticeships continues to be that they let a trainee learn on the job and often in the classroom and earn money while doing so. Still, you need to apply and be accepted to an apprenticeship program before you are let in. This application is similar to a job application. Apprentices are mentored by seasoned pros, and by demonstrating a good work ethic on the job, the apprentice may find their opening their own doors. After all, if a company has just put it a year or more training you, they very well may want to keep their investment. After completing the formal apprenticeship, the trainee rises to the level of journeyman, signifying that he or she is a recognized skilled worker in a trade.

THE TOP TOOLS

No matter what job you want, some tools are universal in the hunting process. The résumé is the main item every job seeker must have. A résumé is a summary of your skills, abilities, and accomplishments, including

The résumé is the job-hunting tool that usually makes the first impression. They need to be clearly laid out and error-free. Go online to research best ways to write a winning résumé.

educational background. The résumé has to be error free and well written.

Other standard job-hunting tools in the employment-finding kit include the cover letter. This is the letter you send to an employer along with your résumé that helps explain why you are applying for the job and why you are an ideal candidate. It's a quick sales pitch for yourself. The cover letter may come with a list of a few people who can be your references. When employers are impressed by a candidate's résumé and cover letter, they often take the next step and call previous employers, who can discuss your work history, strengths, and weaknesses.

When an employer calls you in for an interview, you know you are in the running. To make a good impression, be prepared by practicing your interview skills. Be on time, and afterward send off a thank you note. If you meet with human resources and other staff members of a potential employer, make sure you a dressed right. Putting in the investment to look sharp and dress in such a way that matches the work environment can really pay off.

Any time you're looking for work in this field, make sure you're up to date on the latest trends and tools. This is a job where an ongoing education is necessary to advance.

GLOSSARY

amperes Units of electric current.

breadboard Also called a protoboard, this is a base for pro-
totyping electronics and circuits.

circuit A pathway through which electrical current flows.

current The flow rate of electrons through a circuit, measured in amps.

diagnostics Tests and procedures run on machines to check
if they're performing as they should.

fabrication The act of manufacturing or inventing something.

hydraulics The science and technology of sending liquids
through pipes and channels, especially as a source of
mechanical force or control.

internal combustion engine An engine that generates power
by burning gasoline, oil, or other fuel with air inside the
engine—the hot gases produced drive a piston or do
other work as they expand.

LED lighting Light-emitting diode; an electronic device that
emits light when an electrical current passes through it.

microcontroller A compact microcomputer that may operate a system in a robot, motor vehicle, office machine,
medical device, vending machine, home appliance, or
other device.

millwright A high-precision tradesman who installs, takes
apart, repairs, reassembles, and moves machinery in
factories, power plants, and construction sites.

ohm A measure of resistance to electrical current.

oscilloscope A device for viewing variations in a fluctuating
electrical quantity, which appear temporarily as a visible
wave form on a display screen.

photolithography A standard method for making a printed circuit board (PCB) and microprocessor fabrication.

pneumatics The science and technology of pressurized air—using piped, compressed air resistance to transmit force and energy.

soldering iron A tool for melting solder to join metals.

3D printing A manufacturing process that builds physical objects layer by layer through a high-tech, computer-controlled device; objects can be made from plastic, glass, metal, or ceramic.

transistor A semiconductor device used to amplify or switch electronic signals and electrical power.

voltage A measure of electrical force. It is the push or pressure of the electrons through a circuit.

Association of Information Technology Professionals (AITP)
3500 Lacey Road, Suite 100
Downers Grove, IL 60515
(866) 835–8020
Website: http://www.aitp.org
Facebook and Twitter: @CompTIAAITP
This worldwide society of professionals in information tech-
    nology offers career training, scholarships, news, and
    social networking opportunities.

Canadian Advanced Technology Alliance (CATA)
207 Bank Street, Suite 416
Ottawa, ON K2P 2N2
Canada
(613) 236–6550
Website: http://www.cata.ca
Twitter: @CATAAlliance
The largest high-tech association in Canada, CATA is a
    comprehensive resource of the latest high-tech news
    in Canada.

Canadian Society for Mechanical Engineering
PO Box 40140
Ottawa, ON K1V 0W8
Canada
(613) 400–1786
Website: http://www.csme-scgm.ca
Facebook: @CSMESCGM
Twitter: @CSME_SCGM

A professional organization for Canadian engineers and technologists, the group's site offers sections directed to helping students who pursue mechanical engineering or related programs.

Consumer Electronics Association
1919 S. Eads Street
Arlington, VA 22202
(866) 858–1555
Website: http://www.ce.org
Facebook and Twitter: @CES
This professional group offers news on technology trends and the latest in consumer electronic products.

Nation of Makers
110 University Boulevard, #752
Silver Spring, MD 20918
Website: https://nationofmakers.us
Facebook: @nationofmakers
Twitter: @NationofMakers
This entity is dedicated to the support of the makerspace movement. They unite makerspace organizers around the country and provide resources.

Society of Maintenance and Reliability Professionals
3200 Windy Hill Road SE, Suite 600W
Atlanta, GA 30339
(800) 950–7354
Website: http://www.smrp.org
Facebook: @smrpkco
Twitter: @smrp

This group actively promotes maintenance education and standards. They partner with groups such as the International Council for Machinery Lubrication and other organizations concerned with maintenance technology.

TryComputing.org
445 Hoes Lane
Piscataway, NJ 08854–4141
(732) 981–0060
Website: http://www.trycomputing.org/inspire /computing-student-opportunities
Facebook: @TryEngineering.org
Twitter: @tryengineering
This site from the Institute of Electrical and Electronics Engineers features competitions, events, internships, and research programs for young people. You can also find out about career opportunities and colleges with computer programming courses.

Young Science Canada
1550 Kingston Road, Suite 213
Pickering, ON L1V 1C3
Canada
(866) 341–0040
Website: http://www.youthscience.ca
This organization provides programs to increase awareness and involvement of youth in science, engineering, and technology, to engage, mentor, and recognize Canada's young scientists. Part of their mission is to foster a new generation of innovators, researchers, and entrepreneurs.

FOR FURTHER READING

Boxall, John. *Arduino Workshop: A Hands-on Introduction With 65 Projects*. San Francisco, CA: No Starch Press, 2013.

Brejcha, Lacy. *Makerspaces in School: A Month-by-Month Schoolwide Model for Building Meaningful Makerspace*. Waco, TX: Prufrock Press, 2018.

Carey, Ann. *STEAM Kids: 50+ Science/Technology/Engineering/Art/Math Hands-On Projects for Kid*. North Charleston, SC: Createspace, 2016.

Farrell, Mary. *Computer Programming for Teens*. Boston, MA. Thomas Course Technology, 2008.

Freedman, Jeri. *Careers in Computer Science and Programming*. New York, NY: Rosen Classroom, 2011.

Graves, Colleen. *The Big Book of Makerspace Projects*. New York, NY: McGraw-Hill Education TAB; 1 edition, 2016.

Institute for Career Research. *Career as an Aircraft Mechanic*. North Charleston, SC: Createspace, 2014.

LeBreque, Ellen. *Auto Technician*. North Mankato, MN: Cherry Lake Publishing, 2016.

Orr, Tamra. *A Career as an Auto Mechanic*. New York, NY: Rosen Publishing, 2010.

Rauf, Don. *Getting the Most Out of Makerspaces to Explore Arduino and Electronics*. New York, NY: Rosen Publishing, 2014.

Richardson, Duncan. *Plant Equipment & Maintenance Engineering Handbook*. New York, NY: McGraw-Hill Education, 2018.

BIBLIOGRAPHY

Anderberg, Jeremy. "So You Want My Trade: Automotive Mechanic/Technician." The Art of Manliness, October 29, 2015. https://www.artofmanliness.com/articles /so-you-want-my-tradeautomotive-mechanictechnician.

Bannan, Karen. "Makerspaces Encourage Students to Innovate and Build Critical Thinking Skills." EdTech, October 10, 2016. https://edtechmagazine.com/k12 /article/2016/10/makerspaces-encourage-students -innovate-and-build-critical-thinking-skills.

Bell, Gabriel. "The 12 Best Makerspaces In America Where Kids Learn To Create." Fatherly. Retrieved October 21, 2016. https://www.fatherly.com/play/travel /best-makerspaces-america.

Giffi, Craig. "The Skills Gap in US Manufacturing, 2015– 25." Deloitte. Retrieved October 10, 2018. https:// www2.deloitte.com/us/en/pages/manufacturing /articles/boiling-point-the-skills-gap-in-us -manufacturing.html.

Engineering360. "7 Essentials for Starting A Makerspace." December 20, 2018. https://electronics360.globalspec .com /article/13277/7-essentials-for-starting-a-makerspace.

Hoban, Virgie. "Students in Makerspace Club Design a Robot to Locate Survivors in Disaster." Berkeley Library, September 25, 2018. https://news.lib.berkeley.edu /students-makerspace-club-design-robot-locate -survivors-disaster.

InkSmith. "Makerspaces Are Just the Old Shop Class." Medium, August 3, 2017. https://medium.com

/@InkSmith3D/makerspaces-arejust-the-old-shop-class
-37f162026d38.

Intel. "Careers in Manufacturing." Retrieved October 10,
2018. https://www.intel.com/content/www/us/en/jobs
/careers/manufacturing/technicians.html.

Kaufman, Wendy. "A Successful Job Search: It's All About
Networking." NPR, *All Things Considered*, February 3,
2011. https://www.npr.org/2011/02/08/133474431
/a-successful-job-search-its-all-about-networking.

Lockhart, Charlotte. "Makerspace Movement Is Real." *Sun
Sentinel*, April 10, 2018. http://www.sunsentinel.com
/local/palm-beach/boca-raton/fl-bbf-opinion-mindset
-0411–20180410-story.html.

Makerspaces.com. "What Is a MakerSpace?" Retrieved
October 10, 2018. https://www.makerspaces.com
/what-is-a-makerspace.

Mraz, Stephen. "What's the Difference Between Soldering, Brazing, and Welding?" Machine Design, July 14,
2015. https://www.machinedesign.com/fasteners
/whats-difference-between-soldering-brazing-and
-welding.

Reddit. "We Laser Cut Pickle Rick at My Makerspace."
Retrieved October 10, 2018. https://www
.reddit.com/r/rickandmorty/comments/6t3mnc
/we_laser_cut_pickle_rick_at_my_makerspace.

Rogers, Tony. "Everything You Need to Know About CNC
Machines." Creative Mechanisms, May 20, 2015.
https://www.creativemechanisms.com/blog
/everything-you-need-to-know-about-cnc-machines.

Santa Clarita Gazette. "Advanced Technology Careers for
Students." September 20, 2018. https://santaclaritafree

.com/gazette/community-gazette/advanced-technology
-careers-for-students.

Sofge, Erik. "The World's Top 10 Most Innovative Companies in Robotics." *Fast Company*, February 2, 2014.
https://www.fastcompany.com/3026314/the-worlds
-top-10-most-innovative-companies-in-robotics.

StudyLib. "High School Makerspace Tools & Materials."
April 2012. https://studylib.net/doc/18051515
/april-2012—-maker-education-initiative.

Tierney, John. "How Makerspaces Help Local Economies."
The Atlantic, April 17, 2015. https://www
.theatlantic.com/technology/archive/2015/04
/makerspaces-areremaking-local-economies/390807.

INDEX

R

S

T

U

V

ABOUT THE AUTHOR

Don Rauf is the author of numerous nonfiction books, including *Killer Lipstick and Other Spy Gadgets*, *A Teen's Guide to the Power of Social Networking*, and *Getting the Most Out of Makerspaces to Explore Arduino and Electronics*. He lives in Seattle.

PHOTO CREDITS